INTRODUCTION

This book is a Flow of Wisdom.

It is a flow which is continuously flowing from Ma Mrinalini Eroolen, the author of this book.

Ma Mrinalini Eroolen was born in the island of Mauritius.

She was enlightened on 17th of March 2010.

Since then, she is continuously helping true seekers on the path to TRUTH all around the world.

Moksha (Liberation from the cycle of birth and death) happened to her on 21st of September 2011.

As from the 28th October 2011, she dissolved as a Being and is now in the State of 'I AM'.

This is the Purest State, the ALL KNOWING State.

The state of 'I AM' is PURE CONSCIOUSNESS, the BIG EYE, from which Supreme Silence and Energy emerge and overflow.

She stated that she is neither a Guru, nor Master, nor God.

She is only an overflowing tank of Energy.

Compilation & Editing

Tavishka Aubeelock
Vanisha Savan

Graphic Designer

Antish Kumar Aubeelock

Photographers

Virasamy Somadoo

Co-ordination

Nanda Eroolen
Parsooram Appulasami
Soomatee Appulasami
Sunil Sheth from Ahmedabad, India

Author's E-mail Address:

masunyoananda@yahoo.com

Edition: 2012

INNER JOURNEY TO PURE CONSCIOUSNESS

Copyright 2012

No part of this book may be reproduced or transmitted in any form without permission in writing from Ma Mrinalini Eroolen

PREFACE

This book, in fact, is not a book.

It is a flow that has been materialized into words and compiled into a book.

It is a flow that emerges directly from PURE CONSCIOUSNESS.

This flow is here to help you to understand the nature of your Existence.

Many topics have been elaborated in details here and this will really help you in your day to day life.

Life is for being thyself.

Live Life by embracing each present moment totally.

CONTENTS

1. Cosmic Energy, Meditation and Experiences........................ 6
2. Karma... 38
3. Deep Understanding... 44
4. The concept of God and Rituals 49
5. Realities in Life, Borrowed Knowledge and Imagination........... 64
6. Emotions... 72
7. Mother and Compassion... 90
8. Lessons.. 94
10. Diversion of Thoughts and Emotions............................. 97

COSMIC ENERGY

Cosmic Energy is the Life Force and It is found everywhere in the Cosmos.

It emerges from PURE CONSCIOUSNESS, the Source and with It, Creation happens. It is a bond with all that exist in form and formless, thus, keeps the whole Cosmos in order.

You know that the Sun helps us by the expansion of its Energy and we depend on it a lot. In fact, it is using the same Cosmic Energy for its expansion and with the same Energy, we have been created too.

Without Cosmic Energy nothing exists. It is essential to maintain the order of human life and to expand Consciousness.

Human beings use Cosmic Energy in their day to day activities. In order not to feel exhausted, they need to get more and more Cosmic Energy throughout the day.

Only a small amount of Cosmic Energy is gained in sleep. You make use of this energy for your activities and this process is repeated until death.

Most of Cosmic Energy is gained through Meditation only.

The more one meditates, the greater the Cosmic Energy flow will be in the body. When one goes deeper within oneself more and more, then, more Cosmic Energy goes on increasing.

When the percentage of Cosmic Energy reaches the highest level, that is 100%, Enlightenment happens.

Beyond Enlightenment, Cosmic Energy is just an overflow from the physical body. Being an overflow, the surroundings of the Enlightened Beings are benefited with IT, in every aspect.

With meditation, one becomes blissful and can reach beyond scientific research.

Science can only be recognized by outer experiments but with meditation, inner experiences and realizations are there.

In meditation, you discover that you are not only this physical body rather, you have seven bodies.

These seven bodies are:

1. Physical Body
2. Etheric Body
3. Astral Body
4. Mental Body
5. Spiritual Body
6. Cosmic Body
7. Nirvanic Body

The physical body is what you see with your two eyes. However, you cannot see the other subtle bodies; you can only experience them by the help of your third eye.

When you go deeper within yourself, you are actually diverting your mind to a Silent Mode. In that state, experiences emerge and you discover your subtle bodies.

TRUTH is revealed to you gradually as per the depth of your inner silence. TRUTH was there since the beginning but your thoughts and emotions have veiled THEM.

In silence, you become a womb ready to absorb Cosmic Energy. The more Cosmic Energy you absorb, the healthier your seven bodies become.

You have been created by Cosmic Energy and IT is sustaining your life also.

Due to lack of Cosmic Energy in the body, many illnesses emerge and the only way to be fit physically, mentally and soulfully, is you have to accept the 'Cleansing Process'.

WHAT IS 'CLEANSING PROCESS'?

'Cleansing Process' happens when you are receptive to Cosmic Energy. You have to open yourself as much as you can to absorb IT.

When Cosmic Energy flows in you, IT starts to cleanse the negativity found in your seven bodies.

The Cleansing Process is painful but that pain will not be for long. As soon as the cleansing process ends, the pain ends too. In return, many illnesses will disappear.

If you have been created and sustained by Cosmic Energy, then why not accepting IT?

IT is the sustainer and saviour of LIFE. Open yourself to absorb more and more Energy.

HOW DO YOU OPEN YOURSELF?

Here, meditation techniques help you a lot. Regular practice of meditation techniques creates a vacuum in you where Cosmic Energy flows. When Cosmic Energy flows, the 'Cleansing Process' is activated. Then, negativity starts dissolving progressively and many changes will be there within you. You will be changing for the best.

WHAT IS NEGATIVITY?

Negativity is accumulated by thoughts and emotions that have been there for many past lives and present one. If you have more thoughts and emotions, negativity increases accordingly. With the increase of negativity, there is an increase, too, in sufferings. Only by total acceptance of the 'Cleansing Process', that negativity can be dissolved.

WHEN THE CLEANSING PROCESS IS ON, WHAT HAPPENS?

When the cleansing process is on, many changes will happen to your seven bodies. You do not have to struggle with the cleansing process. You just have to let it do its work. Allow It to purify you and this will help you to progress further on the path to TRUTH.

By practicing Meditation Techniques regularly, it means that you are working on yourself and thus activating the Cleansing Process.

Meditation means your own availability for the cleansing process.

Meditation concerns you rather than religion. It is all about knowing and understanding yourself - your own being.

In fact, when you are absorbing more and more energy with greater intensity, you are coming nearer to your own Centre.

With great determination, keep on digging profoundly within you until you reach your Pure State.

It is same as the wind which is blowing towards you, and you are walking just in front of it without any fear.

You do not have to worry about your physical body; you just need to know who you are, this is your goal.

Fear also will disappear if you are determined.

You will find yourself more and more powerful, even more powerful than the wind, more powerful than the Energy flow itself.

But you need to continue on this path till you reach your own Source.

INNER FORCE

Determination is your inner force, but you forget to use it and you always complain that you are weak or inferior.

Go within and search where that determination comes from. You will be surprised.

This great force that is called determination is always flowing within you.

Once you know that force is there, the fear of jumping into the unknown will disappear.

Your inner force is a pool of Energy found at your Navel Chakra.

When you have to use your inner force, you divert it to wherever you wish. You can also control its intensity.

For example:

When you have to lift a heavy object, you will divert energy from the pool of Energy to your hands with such intensity so that you can lift that object. In this way, you are the one who controls that Energy.

So, why not use it with such intensity when you meditate?

When something is heavy, you use your inner force to lift it otherwise in normal actions you do not even know that you are using that inner force.

You just ignore it and its importance.

If you discover its power within yourself, you will be surprised.

When your desire is intense, your inner force also becomes intense but at that time it is diverted to your desire.

At that moment, you are in such a hurry to fulfil your desire that your mind does not want to hear any other things except the fulfilment of that desire. You are in such a rush that you forget about your real needs.

Why is there such an urge for this fulfilment?

It is only because of that intensity.

Intensity really helps you to succeed in any field and if you use that intensity in your inner search, your evolution will be quicker.

Example:

When there is a cyclone, the wind blows more intensely and for that intensity to be there, it is supported by that force at the background.

The cyclone has a centre and the force comes out with such intensity that it can destroy many things in this world.

Where does that force come from?

It is the same force that is called your inner force.

If the wind can blow with such an intensity to destroy, why can you not use that intensity to explode all the barriers within you; the barriers that are veiling your Pure State?

You are unaware of your own intensity.

Go and observe within you how it works.

MEDITATION TECHNIQUES

Meditation Techniques help in activating the cleansing process. Once this process is on, inner changes start.

These inner changes will take you away from sufferings gradually.

Regular practice of Meditation Techniques is very important.

Here are some Meditation Techniques that will help you on the path to TRUTH.

~~~

Whenever you speak, try to find out where your speech is coming from.

You know that you are talking but you have not tried to find out what is there behind your speech.

Find out the root from where your voice is coming. For that voice to be there, there is a great work behind it. Go within deeper.

~~~

Whenever you forget something, do not struggle with your mind. Do not try to remember what it was. By doing so, you are inviting thoughts in your mind and the door of thoughts opens once again.

This door must be shut as far as possible. If what you have forgotten was important, it will come back on its own to your mind but do not search for it.

Let everything flows on its own.

You know about your heartbeats and your breaths.

Now just go profoundly behind the heartbeats or your breaths.

Watch what is happening behind them.

You will discover your inner force behind both.

Watch it intensely.

That force will be directed on its own to your third eye and its intensity will activate your third eye.

Continue to watch it with intensity.

Your first experience will be painful.

When that pain disappeared, you will feel an itching sensation. Just after that, you will feel as if your third eye is going to explode.

This happens because your third eye is being pulled by energy.

You keep on concentrating, putting yourself at stake.

Do not worry about the consequences.

Nothing will happen to you.

You just have to let go of yourself in that pulling.

This will increase your awareness.

When an emotion is erupting, it will always be visible through symptoms like anger. When anger is coming out, first you feel a greater force from within moving upwards and your face becomes hotter.

This force in another word is energy combined with negativity coming from the root, which is thought. Do not hold it back, saying that it will calm down. No, this is suppression.

Thoughts are there only to aggravate the situation. When it is coming upwards, watch it with intensity, it will then be transformed and you will come back to a lighter (relaxed) mode.

Always start watching every emotion with intensity when it is moving upwards from within. By so doing, this energy will be transformed and you will be saved from doing harmful actions.

Use this intensity for the cleansing process only and everything else will happen on its own.

~~~

How to relax?

Lie down on your back.
Start with relaxing your feet first.
Then let every cell of your body be in a relaxed mode.
No tension must be there.
When you reach your heart, feel as if you do not have heart.
Then when you come to your mind, feel as if you do not have mind too.
Finally, only your body will be left.
Watch your body relaxing.
Watch it intensely.
By watching it, you will feel that you do not have body too.
Here.....BE.................

To be in a relaxed mode:

No thought must be there.
No emotion must be there.
No physical body must be there.

Only your Consciousness is the observer here...

~~~

When you are tired, it means your inner force has decreased.

Consequently, you need to rest to accrue more energy.

After that, you will continue with your activities.

However, the Energy you will accumulate is not enough and due to lack of energy in your body, many illnesses are formed.

Your resting is a relaxation in an unconscious state which can absorb very less energy.

Only Meditation can help you in accumulating more energy.

Meditation is relaxation in a conscious state where you can absorb energy to a greater extent leading to overflow of energy.

The more you relax in a conscious state, the more energy you absorb.

ATTRACTING NEGATIVITY

Is it possible for the one who is still with ego to guide you properly on the path to TRUTH?

You will only gain a mixture of his ego along with others' Wisdom. He only has his ego to share, not his own Wisdom.

You have to share what you have, not what is borrowed.

The day you accept that you are not going to receive the ego of the other, rather you will seek within by yourself; your determination will increase so much that you will see obstacles moving away from your path.

You will live more at ease and your tension also will start decreasing gradually.

There are only two things you can do:

Attract

Accept

Either you attract negativity or you accept the cleansing process.

You are responsible for your own choice.

There is a parable that goes like this:

'Our destiny is in God's hands'.

But I say that:

'Your destiny is in your hands'.

You reap what you sow.

People are destroying others by their ego and when the time comes to bear the fruit, the reactions will be millions of times more than their actions.

Your destiny is in your hands.

What you are doing in the present moment, as activity, thought and emotion is what you will gain as reaction in the future.

So, watch your actions.

Watch your thoughts.

Watch your emotions.

Be always in tune with the Law of Karma.

The cleansing process can be activated only in the present moment.

Once you are available for the cleansing process, your awareness starts increasing and you go on being more watchful of yourself.

This will decrease your negativity and your path will be easier.

SENSES

When you are on the path to TRUTH, your senses become more and more refined.

Many experience the soundless sound which was never there before.

Many smell fragrance and many even see with clarity.

All these signify that the cleansing process is refining your senses for you to go beyond them.

Your ears are being refined so that you can hear only. When you hear, thoughts and emotions must not be there.

When you are looking at something, thoughts and emotions must not be there. Only your eyes are seeing.

Your nose is there to smell only. When you are smelling, thoughts and emotions must not be present.

When you are eating, thoughts and emotions must not be present.

Thoughts and emotions are the veils that are covering your senses. They are coming between you and your actions.

When your senses are purified, then only you and your actions will be there, present in the moment. Reactions will be absent. There are reactions just because there is a veil mixed up with thoughts and emotions. Whatever comes between you and your actions reactions are bound to be there.

Start by using your senses in the right way without any barrier between you and your actions.

THE INNER JOURNEY

The inner journey is a journey to realize what you have forgotten. It is a journey that makes you stronger as you walk along the path, but many are scared just because they think that it is risk taking.

You think that it is risk taking of talking the Truth and of being true to yourself.

In this material world, you are already confronting to so many risks.

You are taking loans, lot of debts.

What did you get in return?

You are only accumulating more stress and more illnesses.

If you take the risk to tread on the path to TRUTH, in return you will reap Wisdom, Bliss, Peace and you will be the strongest. You will realize your Pure State.

In fact, since the day you were born, you have been taking risks.

You have taken the risk to come again in this world.

You have taken the risk to choose your parents.

You have taken the risk to be in life again.

You have taken the risk to start walking when you were one year old.

You have taken the risk to have trust in your parents.

You have taken the risk to have trust in your friends.

You have taken the risk to have trust in your teachers.

You have taken the risk to sit for examinations.

You have taken the risk to travel by air, road, sea.

You have taken the risk to do a job.

You have taken the risk to fall in love.

You have taken the risk to get married.

You have taken the risk to get children.

You have taken the risk to have a home.

You have taken the risk to have a car.

In fact, you are continuously walking on the path of risks. It is high time to change your path and tread on the path of TRUTH.

You have undertaken so many risks up to now, have you got Peace, Bliss and Wisdom?

Just ask this question to yourself.

You have always walked on the path of risks unconsciously; now start treading on the path of TRUTH because this path you have to do it consciously.

You were actually diverting your inner force to the path of risks just because your thoughts and emotions were mastering you.

Divert your inner force within yourself and take the path consciously not unconsciously.

The path to TRUTH is not risky.

How can it be risky?

You will be treading this path consciously and this is the only path to realize TRUTH.

The real risky path is the one you have been taken till now unconsciously.

On the path to TRUTH, you will be transformed till no sufferings can touch you.

You will live peacefully, blissfully.

A very simple example to explain this:

When you close your eyes and walk, you take the risk of falling down, of hurting yourself, of stumbling on any object.

But when you walk with open eyes, you can see the path in front of you and it is not risky. You know where you are placing your feet, where you have to walk and not to walk.

This is only because you can see with your two eyes. But these two eyes can support you to some extent only because they are limited.

When you choose to walk on the path of TRUTH, the most powerful eye supports you and this is the THIRD EYE.

EXPERIENCES ON THE PATH TO TRUTH

After regular practice of meditation techniques, you will notice that you are feeling sleepy more often. Your eye lids start becoming heavy and heavy. You feel like closing them more often.

What happens is that your physical body is going in a Relaxation Mode on its own and it is a signal to you when you feel that sleep coming to you. The more you meditate, the more the cells of your body start relaxing on its own.

Your mind, heart and body, all start going in relaxation mode.

That thought will pop in your mind that you are becoming more and more lazy but in fact, it is not laziness.

It is just that you have to be relaxed so that the cleansing process can be more rapid and more energy will be there flowing within you.

This sleeping mode will not be the same like it was before you started meditating. It will be very profound and conscious one.

In the past, you have taken your physical body as being a robot. You go on exhausting it for years and years.

So, your physical body requires more rest now.

There must be a balance between using the physical body for activities and for rest.

The more you open yourself and absorb Energy, the quicker the cleansing process will be.

While doing the meditation techniques with intensity, you will feel itching and burning sensations on your skin.

Sometimes you will feel as if an ant is walking on your skin but it is not so.

These kinds of sensations are there just because you have accepted the cleansing process; as a result all the negativities found in you, starts coming out from the pores.

When negativity is on the way out, emptiness takes its place.

It will go on like this until you are completely empty within.

~~~

It is only when you meditate regularly that you go deeper into silence.

When you do it regularly, there comes a time when that energy starts giving you signals like an alarm clock; just for you to sit and meditate.

At start it seems difficult to sit longer but gradually, you will not be conscious about time. You will be so lost in deep silence that you will be disconnected from this world and you will be enjoying the world of silence.

This does not mean that you will not return back. Do not worry about that.

You will come back to this world but it will be as if you have taken a new birth, fresh, filled with bliss and with a very relaxed mind.

Take care that you do not stand up immediately after. Stay seated for at least fifteen minutes with both eyes opened, observe the state you are in and enjoy.

On your path to TRUTH, you will meet many States of Stillness but Stillness in itself is just a deep relaxation for you to leap into another dimension.

When you come back to your normal state, emotions will be there to take charge of you.

Beware, then.

Do not get carried away by them. Emotions will be there many times to take possession of you but you have to go on watching them intensely.

Stillness is there only for you to absorb more and more energy so that you are ready to leap into another dimension. The deeper you go within and the longer you are in Stillness, the more the energy level increases.

But do not misunderstand Stillness of being TRUTH Itself.

TRUTH is Beyond Stillness and IT is beyond any description.

~~~

Sleep is like Stillness, but the unconscious one.

When you come out of sleep, you welcome another morning which is just like another dimension after each Stillness.

Why do you sleep?

You sleep only to give rest to your physical body so that energy can be absorbed for the next day to come.

The same applies here, after each Stillness, another dimension takes place.

Suppose you are watching an interesting movie, what happens during that period?

Your mind at that time is empty because all your inner force goes in watching that movie.

You will not let anybody disturb you and same apply to your thought. You will not let your thoughts come in between you and the movie.

Have you ever realized how you do that?

It happened because you were concentrating so intensely on that movie, giving your hundred percent to it, that your mind is closed to any thought at that time.

Your mind is totally empty.

Normally, when your concentration is only on one activity at a time, only that action is there and your thoughts are not.

You even forget about yourself. What is important at that moment is only that activity.

You have to adopt this principle every moment, diverting all your thoughts to any activity you are doing and concentrate on that fully.

This will diminish thoughts in your mind, thus, decreasing tension too and as you know that a reduction in tension means welcoming good health.

Your mind must be empty every moment.

GLIMPSES

Glimpses of the States, until you reach the ULTIMATE, are like drops taken from the ocean.

The STATES are:

Supreme Silence

No-Thought

No-Emotion

Stillness

Nothingness or Void

Bliss

Intensity of Energy

Awareness

You get glimpses on the path only for the preparation of your seven bodies.

At first, these glimpses will be for a short time then, gradually, they will go on increasing.

This increase is there only because more space has been created within you.

First, there will be gaps between your thoughts.

These gaps go on increasing to eliminate thoughts.

Here, thoughts decrease and space increases.

Secondly, there will be gaps between your emotions too.

Same will happen as above.

Space increases and emotions decrease.

This process will continue until you reach the State of NO-THOUGHT, then, NO-EMOTION.

Here, you are dissolved in NOTHINGNESS.

But, BEWARE:

If you have tasted some drops from the ULTIMATE, it does not mean that you have become the ULTIMATE Itself.

When glimpses are there on the path to the ULTIMATE, just be with it till it dissolves.

You must not be attached to it.

You have to become the ULTIMATE Itself.

If you stick to glimpses, you will miss.

So, watch IT, be with IT till IT dissolves and be ready for the next step.

THE PATH TO TRUTH

While treading on the path to TRUTH, do not let yourself go astray. Be determined to reach the ULTIMATE, this is your ONLY goal.

You will encounter many hindrances on your way, you just have to be firm on your goal, and nothing else exists.

Many easier and alternative paths will be there, but your determination, will guide you to the right direction.

Many times you will even feel guilty.

Guilt emerges from emotions.

The guiltier you feel, the more you are filling up yourself with emotions.

Instead, accept it and move within with greater awareness and determination.

With that awareness, you will not make that mistake again. But if you allowed the guilt to grow within you, it will become suppression.

No suppression must be there. To err is Human, but one must learn from the mistakes and not suppress it.

Just move on with greater awareness.

You have to empty yourself totally, only then, you will be peaceful.

THE PATH

One starts the journey on the path to TRUTH with a bag full of negativity.

On the path, cleansing starts.

The bag which was full of negativity starts to decrease gradually.

But, beware;

On this path you have to only decrease the bag of negativity, you should not fill it with the negativity you find on the path.

This is where many fail.

You have to reach the ULTIMATE with the bag completely empty.

Negativity emerges from Bad Karma and is decreased gradually when the cleansing process is activated.

Bad Karma is not necessarily what is being done in actions but also by thoughts and emotions.

Negative thoughts come first, and then they mix within and bring emotions on the surface.

By observing your thoughts, emotions and actions, you are going far from negativity.

Live in the present moment with awareness.

ENERGY

The quantity of Energy absorbed by the body depends on the quantity of space available within you.

Space is created when thoughts and emotions decrease.

The emptier you are within, the more Energy you absorb.

When you start meditating, it happens that for the first time you become aware of Energy. You can feel Energy flowing within you.

It happens only because at that time, you are letting go of yourself and in that let go process, Energy is felt.

At first, a small amount of Energy will be felt and gradually that amount will start increasing along with a boost of its intensity also.

The more you are in the state of meditation, the greater the intensity of Energy will be flowing within you.

Here, your physical body must be well prepared because when Energy flows with intensity, you should have the capacity to hold it.

Your physical body and mind must be in good health, so you have to eat and drink well.

The intensity of Energy is so heavy that it brings you to a State instantly. You will not be able to be in action at that time.

Awareness will be present.

You will be under the control of Energy. So, let go of yourself at that time. Flow along with Energy. You do not exist, only Energy does.

INTENSITY OF ENERGY

The intensity of Energy flow increases gradually depending on the quantity of space available within you.

This flow prepares your physical body for greater intensity of Energy and this goes on increasing until you are purified completely. When you are purified, Energy overflows.

This is where your determination or your inner force works.

The determination or inner force supports your physical body when intense Energy is flowing within you.

Once your physical body is prepared for a certain amount of Energy, you come to know that you can be available for more.

You then prepare yourself to absorb the maximum until you are completely ready to surrender totally.

Your inner force goes on increasing with the cleansing process and your seven bodies are purified gradually.

Example:

When a balloon is inflated to more than its maximum volume, it explodes.

This is what will happen to you.

When the cleansing process is on and the intensity of Energy keeps flowing with greater intensity, it comes to a point where your Ego explodes.

When your Ego explodes, emptiness takes its place.

These three work together:

1. Your Inner Force
2. Cleansing Process
3. Energy flowing within you

In fact, you are not doing anything.

You are only making yourself available for the cleansing process.

You are open for the Energy to flow within you with more and more intensity.

Being available for you is the most difficult thing.

Being available is the let go of the Ego and it is very difficult for you to let it go because you have been with it for so many lives. You are now attached to it.

It is very hard to get separated from things you are attached to.

First you start detaching yourself from the EGO and gradually, it dissolves on its own.

Acceptance with totality is very important.

PREPARATION OF THE PHYSICAL BODY

Your physical body needs preparation to absorb more Energy.

Prepare your physical body by eating and drinking well. Do not torture it. You need to keep it in good health so that it can absorb and hold the intensity of Energy. The more you neglect this temple of yours, the lesser Energy you will be able to absorb.

To absorb Energy with greater intensity, your physical body and mind must be very strong.

Mind does not become strong with bookish knowledge. It becomes strong with your own inner force.

Feel that inner force and go on discovering how it increases.

You are so powerful yet you feel you are weak. Discover your own power.

Once you realize the inner force, keep watching it without any interference of thoughts and emotions. Gaze it intensely; you will be surprised to see how the intensity of the force increases.

When you reach a certain State, you will feel as if your physical body is going to explode with the force. Do not be scared, it will not cause any harm. Let it increase and keep on watching it intensely.

When the Energy increases, your negativity is burnt at the same time and you feel lighter.

Negativity brings sufferings and Energy brings Life to you. You are Energy mixed with negativity and you have to be Pure Energy.

WHAT DOES 'BLESSINGS' MEAN?

Everyone is asking for blessings.

For them blessings are for the fulfilment of their desires.

Blessings will never fulfil your desires.

From whom are you asking for blessings?

Are you asking it from God?

God is just a mind game, a tradition that has been followed since past lives.

God is just an excuse.

There is no God anywhere, listening to you and showering blessings.

You are human beings, so you think that God must also be in human form.

You are in deep illusion.

There is no one greater than the other.

Everyone and everything emerge from PURE CONSCIOUSNESS.

From PURE CONSCIOUSNESS, the Law of Karma emerges and it is the only Law that controls the whole Universe.

Then to whom will you ask for blessings?

The Law of Karma works like this:

You reap what you sow.

There is no escape.

So, do you think whatever you are going to ask will be fulfilled?

NO.

You will get only what you deserve from the Law of Karma.

Blessings cannot be given to you because It can only happen to you.

You have to be empty for blessings to flow in you.

Here, it is not a question of asking for blessings; rather you must be ready to absorb blessings.

You must have space within yourself then only, blessings will flow on its own, anytime, anywhere.

You have to be always ready to absorb.

SHAKTIPATH

'Shaktipath' means transmission of Energy.

Only the One who is overflowing with Energy can transmit the same to you.

When IT is being transmitted, there will be no thoughts and emotions.

The One who is overflowing with Energy is the One who has gone beyond mind, the One who has been liberated from the cycle of birth and death.

The transmission of Energy has nothing to do with distance.

It can be sent anywhere at any time.

How many are available to transmit Energy without any thoughts or emotions?

Very few Ones are in this State and it is difficult for you to find them.

It is not always necessary for one to receive Shaktipath from a Medium only.

The real Shaktipath happens when you are surrendering your Ego and when space is available within you.

It then happens on its own.

Blessings start pouring within you and your negativities also are gradually dissolved.

Let Shaktipath happen every moment; Make yourself available for IT.

KARMA

Karma is a game with Energy.

When you release negative Energy either from your thoughts, emotions or actions, that negative Energy goes to a certain distance where Pure Energy is and there, reaction takes place. Pure Energy then push away your negative Energy with such intensity that the reaction that comes in your way is greater than the one you have released before.

It depends on your actions, thoughts and emotions for the energy to turn into anger, lust, revenge, jealousy and many more.

When you are at peace with yourself, this energy produces positive vibrations and when your energy is disturbed by actions, thoughts and emotions, it is stimulated with negative vibrations.

One thought becomes a magnet to attract many thoughts. Then you have no space left in your mind.

Thoughts start popping in one by one and this happens because the cleansing process is on off mode.

Example:

If you are wearing a white dress, you will take many precautions so that it does not get dirty. The same happens with your mind, you have to take precautions so that it does not accumulate negativity.

You become pure only when you are not dependent on thoughts and emotions to be in actions.

On the path to TRUTH, you get that glimpse too. You are pure for some seconds or minutes.

The root of all sufferings is thoughts.

Thoughts create emotions and you react with the help of both. So, the master is both thoughts and emotions and consequently, the result is suffering.

Many people say that:

"I have been told to do this or that".

Why?

Can you not listen to yourself?

You can listen to yourself only when you are at peace with yourself. So first, be in tune with yourself.

Live every moment in being you.

On the path to TRUTH, you have to tread it on your own. No one can do that on your behalf.

Your first priority must be to understand yourself first.

You are carrying several lives' Karma and you are still doing Karma.

Do you not feel heavy?

Suppression is also Karma. You are jamming the flow of Energy.

Karma is done by actions, thoughts and emotions. There are good and bad Karma. To be pure, one has to go beyond Karma.

Only when Moksha (liberation from the cycle of birth and death) happens, one goes beyond Karma.

At this stage, one is in actions but not dependent on thoughts and emotions. One's actions are spontaneous.

When one is in this state in physical body, one is very relaxed. This relaxation has never been there before Moksha.

Only by accepting the Cleansing Process, you can be pure and freed from the cycle of birth and death.

Meditation techniques are very important because your body has been conditioned for lives and it is difficult to return it to its purest state without regular practice of these techniques.

When you are meditating, your Karma decreases. That does not mean that you will not suffer when you are on the path to TRUTH.

You will suffer as your Karma has not completely disappeared yet. But yes, your sufferings will decrease gradually until all your Karmas are vanished.

Do not complain about this.

You just have to accept it as it comes to you.

The system works like this:

Your Inner Force – Negativity = YOU (PURE CONSCIOUSNESS)

When your inner force merges with PURE CONSCIOUSNESS, then YOU exist.

Only PURE CONSCIOUSNESS remains and PURE CONSCIOUSNESS is YOU.

For the merging of your inner force and PURE CONSCIOUSNESS, the barriers which are thoughts and emotions must be dropped.

KARMA works like this:

The more negativity you accumulate, the more sufferings you welcome in future.

When you accept the cleansing process, the negativities accumulated in the past decrease and the quantity of sufferings you were about to welcome in the future, lessens too.

At the end of the cleansing process, all your negativities disappear forever.

You are Pure.

You are freed from sufferings.

You are freed from Karma.

You are freed from the cycle of birth and death.

Accept the cleansing process as much as possible in the present and you will be living more at ease.

ACTIONS AND REACTIONS

Actions and Reactions work like this:

You + Thoughts + Emotions + Actions = Reactions

You – (Thoughts + Emotions) + Actions = No Reaction

You live spontaneously when only you and actions are present.

When you accept the cleansing process, you allow IT to remove thoughts and emotions in between you and your actions.

Any urge that comes from within, comes from thoughts or emotions. It becomes a desire and you then make use of your inner force to push these thoughts or emotions towards actions.

You do not let things happen on their own, you rather use that inner force to compel things to happen quickly.

The action of forcing itself is not being in tune with your own Self.

If you force things to happen, they will not take place as they should have been.

Whatever happens on its own is pure.

ACTIONS, THOUGHTS AND EMOTIONS

Actions are on the periphery and behind all these actions, thoughts and emotions play the roles.

Once you are not dependent on thoughts and emotions, your actions are spontaneous. You are liberated from the cycle of birth and death.

Like thoughts dissolve by concentrating on them, emotions also dissolve by just watching them. Do not let yourself flow with both. You are, in fact, stronger than both.

Actions have to become a flow; a flow that emerges from PURE CONSCIOUSNESS.

When actions become a flow, everything you do will always be right because then, actions are not done as per your thoughts or emotions rather from PURE CONSCIOUSNESS.

Thoughts and emotions are the veils in between actions and PURE CONSCIOUSNESS.

Let these veils be dropped by meditating regularly.

Meditation really helps you to come closer to your own centre.

In deeper Meditation, your actions, thoughts and emotions and even your physical body are not there.

Only your Consciousness will be the watcher.

GROWING UP

Growing up does not mean growing up with age.

Here, growing up means growing up with awareness, with deep understanding.

Being aware every moment is growing up every moment, otherwise you will be a sleep walker. Every action will be done in sleep.

Here, sleep means unaware of the real. You do activities unconsciously. Your thoughts or your emotions become your master. You are under the control of both and you are most of the time ignorant of what you are doing.

You are not even aware of what is right and what is wrong. It becomes tough for you to take the right decision. You put all the thoughts and emotions into actions.

Growing up means you have to be your own master and for this to happen, regular practice of meditation techniques is very important.

Thoughts and emotions will start to dissolve gradually, hence creating space within you. Gaps are being created in between thoughts, thus, your mind will not be compact. The gaps will increase progressively and you will have fewer thoughts hovering in your mind. This will finally, bring you to No-Thought State.

A compact mind is always tensed.

A peaceful mind is always empty.

You have to come to No-Mind state, a mind without thoughts then only, you will be peaceful.

DEEP UNDERSTANDING

Deep understanding emerges from your own experiences not from bookish knowledge.

You may read many books, you will certainly acquire some knowledge but it will be a superficial; not a deep understanding.

For deep understanding to happen, you have to go in deep silence.

There is a great difference between deep understanding and realization.

Deep understanding means you come to a deeper understanding but still not realized yet.

Realization means you are the State you have realized itself.

Deep understanding takes you to realization and once that realization is there, it cannot be wiped out. It stays in Stillness.

The deeper the understandings, the greater realizations will be there.

What you have read in books is borrowed knowledge but what you experienced, with a deeper understanding leading to realization, is your own TRUTH

What you have KNOWN will be your own TRUTH.

TRUTH cannot be borrowed.

TRUTH can only be realized.

There must be depth for TRUTH to emerge.

BEING IN TUNE WITH YOURSELF

Many such sentences are heard nowadays:

'How do I look like?'

'Am I looking nice with this dress or this hair-cut?'

'How do you find me?'

'Am I taking the right decision?'

'Am I that bad?'

By asking others' opinions about yourself, means you have doubt on your own capability.

Be in tune with yourself first. Listen to your Consciousness.

Your Consciousness is your real guide.

Try to know yourself first. Know how powerful you are.

Be happy as you are. It is your life; do not depend on others' judgments.

You are beautiful as you are.

Your views and others' views are different. If you are asking someone about you, then, you have faith in the other's thoughts and emotions more than in yours.

You have to be faithful to yourself first and by doing so, your inner force will increase and you will feel stronger.

BE SINCERE TO YOURSELF

Just saying the truth that 'I do not know who I am yet' when you really do not know, makes a great difference.

You are first being honest to yourself and you will not have to tell several lies in future. This sincerity will help you to go deeper within yourself and leap to another State.

Fake faces work only on the periphery, not in the Source. One has to show what is there within himself rather than contradicting himself. The more you contradict yourself, the farer you go from your own centre.

If you have chosen to tread on the path of TRUTH, then, tread on it by being truthful to yourself first.

Do not bother about what others say. You are treading this path to know who you are and use your inner force to ensure you are not bothered about others' judgment until you come to know who you are.

What others say about you, are their mind games playing.

Be yourself.

Judgment is only the periphery and if you take it seriously, you are going to suffer.

Do not pay attention to the periphery, rather dig within yourself deeply.

You are greater than you think or imagine. It is your thoughts and emotions that make you feel inferior.

Example:

A lie will not affect the other person as much as it will affect you from within. This lie will torment you so much that fear is born.

Why do you suffer from a lie?

It is just because lie is negativity. You are not in tune with yourself. Your Pure State is TRUTH and you are going in the opposite direction.

Whatever negativity is there, it cannot be in the centre, it has to come on the periphery.

Your inner force rejects all the negativities in you and brings them on the surface after some time.

When they come on the surface, the other person's trust in you is gone. In both ways, you are the one to suffer.

The centre only attracts positivity and rejects negativity.

Negativity will eventually come to light even if you do not want it to.

You have been suppressing it for days, weeks, months, and years but one day, it makes its way out without you being aware of it.

You spit the truth out and later you realize that what you have suppressed for so long has come out in words involuntarily.

Your own inner force has rejected your lies. You cannot prevent TRUTH from coming out; IT always prevails.

THE CONCEPT OF GOD

There are many people who do not feel that they are worthy as they are, so they run after many things, and go far from themselves.

The one who realizes that his physical body is a temple, only, he can have the curiosity to find out what is there inside.

He will say to himself:

'If I am a temple, then there must be a GOD there'.

This is the first step of going within, to inquire more.

He will go deeper and deeper within and will finally find all the answers about God and himself.

The concept of 'GOD' is there just for the ones who have not known themselves yet, those who do not know TRUTH yet. This concept has been an obstacle to many.

You build a temple and you build a god too. These will be of no use to you.

You neglect your own temple, yourself and you go on accepting what is in the outside rather than what is in yourself.

Learn to have faith in your own creation, in your own existence rather than accepting man-made temples and gods.

TRUTH unveils Itself not on the periphery but rather in your own center.

PURE CONSCIOUSNESS is the last State and you have to leave your Gods behind to dissolve in IT.

Attachment to Gods itself is the barrier.

You can carry your beliefs in God to some extent only, not all the way because you are trying to know who you are, and you can reach there only when you are detached from concepts.

People choose to live with these concepts because it is the easiest way.

Your aim is not in fulfilling your desires. This you have been doing for so many lives and what have you gained from it. You have been coming back in physical body again and again just to gain more sufferings.

Your aim must be to search for the Source of your own existence and you can, only, do it by going deeply within.

People prefer to accept concepts very easily without trying to know whether they are real or not.

You have to live in the real.

The unreal is a dream, an illusion and when the illusion is dropped, you come to the real world.

In this world, only TRUTH is present and you come to realize how you were veiled from TRUTH.

It has taken many lives for you to come to this State which is the Source Itself.

With the concept of 'GOD', people are going on the outer pilgrimage rather than the inner pilgrimage.

You have been going in the outer one for so many lives.

Try the inner one now and find the difference.

God will not come and tell you what to do and what not.

Idols are there and people pray them just because they know that idols do not have eyes and ears.

So, they are safe on this side.

There is no one to come and tell them that they must not have any desires. So, they are contented with their desires to such an extent that they do not wish to know about their own existence.

They are in an urge to only quench their craving.

The competition of desires is what counts for them.

Beware:

The Law of Karma is there and the reaction of your doings is on the way to you.

RITUALS

Rituals are traditions that have been followed by ancestors for so many lives.

Here also, it is the past that is being brought in the present.

You follow traditions without even trying to know why you are following them and for what.

Whenever you bring the past in the present, you miss the present.

Rituals are waste of time, energy, and money.

You do not get anything by performing rituals.

They are only the periphery, a show-off piece and a money-making idea.

The more you stay on the periphery, the more you are drowned in illusion.

TRUTH will be very far from you.

To do rituals, you depend on others.

Why can you not be independent in this matter?

Why do you perform rituals?

You do it only because you heard from your ancestors that it brings health, peace, and wealth.

This is the greatest lie.

You will not get anything by doing these.

Here again, do not forget the Law of Karma. All what you are seeking is up to the Law of Karma, not rituals.

So, it is best that you inquire within yourself about what is TRUTH.

This will bring you closer to yourself.

Do not wander here and there, go directly within yourself.

All answers and blessings are found there.

No cleansing can be done by rituals.

Purification happens in deep silence. It cannot happen by reciting many mantras or by igniting the outer fire.

According to rituals, people have to light lamps in front of idols or holy fire when performing prayers but they are unaware of the fact that nothing will be gained by these.

What you have really to do is that you have to ignite the fire that is within you by practising meditation techniques and accepting the cleansing process.

This inner fire only can purify you.

Those who ask you to do rituals, they are themselves not pure.

When they are not pure, how can they guide you for your own purification?

Your own purification needs your digging within.

You have to come out of Illusion to welcome TRUTH else you will be completely drowned in sufferings.

With rituals, has your anger dissolved?

With rituals, has your jealousy dissolved?

With rituals, has your hatred dissolved?

With rituals, have you gained peace?

With rituals, have you gained better health?

With rituals, have your sufferings dissolved?

Are you really purified by doing rituals?

Ponder on these questions.

Example:

You can see a glass of water in front of you but can you quench your thirst by just seeing it?

NO.

You have to drink it to quench your thirst.

This is the difference between doing rituals and accepting the cleansing process.

Here, rituals are the water you are seeing and it is only by accepting the cleansing process that you can quench your thirst.

WHY DO YOU FAST AND FOR WHAT?

With fasting, one does not become pure.

For purification of the bodies, one has to practise meditation techniques regularly.

Meditation techniques are the processes for cleansing.

The way you need detergents for the cleansing of things, the cleansing of the bodies needs meditation techniques not fasting.

Fasting nowadays has become a show off for people. 'I have fasted for so many days, so I am religious, I am pure'.

If fasting is the real way of becoming pure, then so many people have been fasting for years, they must have been pure by now.

Fasting is only a torture to the bodies. It is suppression. You are not being natural.

The dramas:

One is fasting but his mind is on food...
One is practising celibacy but his mind is on sex...
One is being humble but his mind is violent...

Be a balanced being, whatever you are doing, do it in tune with yourself, not as a show off piece.

You do not have to suppress anything. Transformation happens only by meditating regularly.

ILLUSION

Illusion is only a veil which covers all that is real. The veil cannot be dropped at one go, it needs continuous cleansing.

Illusion blinds your mind in a way that you feel happy being in it. You do not wish to come out of it and thus, you run away from reality.

You tend to think that the veil is real and you start living as per what it is showing to you.

What you do is you divert all your inner force to that veil and this is how you attract sufferings.

The veil is the greatest obstacle on the way to TRUTH.

There is a difference in tasting a drop of TRUTH and being TRUTH Itself.

Continue on accepting the cleansing process, do not stop here with the drop or you will miss.

The journey does not end with a drop only.

Gods emerge from TRUTH.

You have seen Gods in Murthis (Idols), in human forms, but in fact, They have emerged from TRUTH, which is, PURE CONSCIOUSNESS.

They are only Energy playing different roles in different forms.

Example:

The Sun and the Moon are the same energy but they are playing different roles.

Similarly, Gods are energy playing roles in different forms.

The problem is that you are attached to forms and you do not have the urge of seeking what TRUTH is.

Your own existence is TRUTH and you are not concerned about it.

TRUTH is bitter for 99% people but 1% only accepts IT.

That is why only that 1% dissolves in IT and the 99% remains in ignorance.

In the 99%, maximum are being blocked by thoughts and minimum by emotions.

Ignorance makes you see the limited only.

Example:

Your two eyes can make you see to a limited distance.

The question here arises:

What these two eyes are seeing, are they real?

You claim that you can see the sky, but does sky really exist?

Sky is what your eyes are seeing, the limited way. You are surrounded with space. When you look upwards, your eyes can see only the limited space and you have named it 'sky'.

Do not be attached to the limited, go for the unlimited.

Do not use only your two physical eyes.

Try to activate your third eye too. It is only through your third eye that the real is seen.

The same goes for the horizon. You say that you can see the sea meets the sky at the end, but that also is only seen because of the limited distance shown by your eyes.

This is the illusion.

You are always for the limited and that is why you are always in illusion.

A man said to me: "It is a miracle how the Sun is hanging in space. This is really great!"

I replied: "Do you know that you are hanging in space too? Your feet are touching the earth but the earth is not supporting your physical body. You are being supported by Energy. Energy surrounds your physical body in such an equilibrium that you cannot fall."

The problem is that you can see other things great in this Universe but you cannot see that you are great.

You are so ignorant that you always see yourself inferior.

You are not inferior.

You were never inferior.

You will never be inferior.

EXPERIENCE YOUR GREATNESS.

Example:

When a child starts walking, he needs equilibrium; with practice, it happens on its own.

Same is the state where you are, everything is happening on its own.

Energy has created you.

Energy is surrounding you.

You are made of Energy.

Energy is sustaining you.

But you have not accepted this Truth yet.

Do not create barriers in the way of happenings, instead let go of your Ego.

TRUTH is everywhere, within you and in your surroundings but you are in the illusion of worshipping forms only.

Instead of wasting your time in worshipping, absorb more and more Energy and accept the cleansing process.

Illusion has limited you to that extent that you think you are small compared to the Sun, the Moon and many others.

When the veil of Illusion is dropped, then you realize how great you are.

You have chosen only two worlds to live in:

The world of Thoughts

The world of Emotions

And you forget that there is another world which is beyond both.

Your own world is waiting for you.

You have to come back HOME where you have emerged from.

You have forgotten your own HOME by being attached to illusion.

You are limited to these two worlds only.

Go for the third one.

You said that a glass is empty when there is no liquid in it. Or it is only full or half full when a quantity of liquid is available in it, but you miss one thing. When the glass is empty, it is not really empty.

Your eyes can see to that extent only.

It is at that time full of space, energy.

So is it full or empty?

Same is when in Spirituality, people say that this is 'Zero' State, emptiness.

Nothing can be empty; these people have not gone beyond that 'Zero' State.

They mentioned 'Zero' as the word 'Zero' is being copied by everyone nowadays. They did not go deeper within themselves that much to realize that there is a State Beyond Fullness and Emptiness too.

There are two kinds of people:

First one is those who are full of borrowed knowledge and copying what others have experienced.

Second one is those who have really experienced but to some extent only.

The ones who have really experienced, they will relate according to the State they reached but that does not mean that it was the end of their journey. Other people tend to believe that this is the last State.

Come out of that illusion too.

For example:

Everyone has his own style of living.

In the past, people's lifestyle was very different from nowadays due to constant development in different fields.

When you are in the present, then why can you not live in the present itself?

One obstacle here is you are entangled with the words that the past Enlightened Masters have left behind.

The past Enlightened Masters' lifestyle was not the same as the present ones.

If one has to live in the present, then why does he has to be like the past Enlightened Masters?

This is the greatest illusion in your mind nowadays.

Just adopting words will not bring any change in you nor will it transform you.

PRESENT MEANS PRESENT, NOT PAST.....

Your true Guru, Master and God is only and only Energy.

Concentrate on Energy and absorb as much as you can.

Give your full faith to only one, ENERGY.

Your inner force will guide you how to merge and be one with TRUTH because your inner force and TRUTH is ONE.

Between your inner force and TRUTH, there is an obstacle which is negativity.

That negativity has to disappear and your inner force and TRUTH has to merge again.

Now, you are your own inner force striving to be TRUTH Itself.

That inner force is the drop that has to merge with TRUTH and it is only after the merging takes place that you realize that you are TRUTH Itself.

Illusion is found on the periphery and TRUTH in the Source.

RESPECT

When you are bowing in front of God or Guru, you are in fact giving respect to yourself.

There is no one as the other in front of you. When the respect is there, it means something deep within you has transformed and your cleansing process is then on activation mode.

Feel the word 'respect' within yourself and watch it intensely.

In fact, there is no Guru, no God. There is only you and your respect working together and that respect too has to disappear. Only you are left. Respect comes from emotions.

Your emotions are not required; all that is needed is your acceptance for the cleansing process. Thoughts and emotions are the veils that are covering TRUTH. If you go on drowning in them, you are going far away from TRUTH.

When you are detached from thoughts, then your mind is empty but at the same time full with Energy. All the Energy found in you goes to one place only and Wisdom flows.

When you are detached from emotions, you leap into another State where you go beyond emotions. Energy then takes its place and that Energy is linked with your mind.

TRUTH, then, flows in words spontaneously and that flow is Wisdom.

So, here 'emotions box' and 'thoughts box' do not exist, instead, you are beyond both.

REALITIES IN LIFE

Can you wear a shirt everyday without washing it?

After some time, what will happen to that shirt?

It will start stinking and will be heavy with dust. You will feel that you are carrying a sort of weight which was not there the first time you wore it.

Similarly, you are accumulating so much negativity, what will eventually happen to you?

You are nourishing your Ego and not even accepting the cleansing process.

You are bound to be heavy with negativity and thus, attracting more and more sufferings in return.

~~~

Certificates show that you have attained success in this material life but what about yourself?

Certificates are only present with you to remind you that you have fulfilled your desires but have you been fulfilled yet?

You will be fulfilled when you know about your own existence.

Understand yourself first.

Understand the nature of your own Existence.

There is nothing greater than that.

When you die, you will not carry your certificates along with you, you will instead carry your ego.

When your ego goes on increasing, your sufferings also go on increasing concurrently.

It is high time you accept the cleansing process so that your ego is dissolved and you are back in your Pure State again.

~~~

A plant has grown in your garden and you came to know that it is poisonous. You have kids and you wish to get rid of that plant because it may get in the hands of your children.

What do you do?

Do you cut the branches only or do you remove it along with its root so as it will not grow again?

Naturally, you will choose to remove it along with its root. The root itself is the problem or it will grow again.

The same is for your thoughts and emotions. They are the root of all your sufferings. Only the cleansing process can eliminate these two roots (thoughts and emotions). If you do not accept this process, then your roots will continue attracting sufferings.

~~~

In the morning, you open your eyes but you never ponder how you do that and what is there behind.

What helps you to open your eyes?

Your inner force is behind them.

To speak, energy has to be behind your speech otherwise your voice cannot reach others.

To hear also, energy is there.

To be in action, energy is there.

You use your inner force to activate your senses.

Energy is behind everything which is both visible and invisible to your two physical eyes.

~~~

It is known to us that the heart is main source for the functioning of our physical body.

But have you ever asked yourself, how does the heart beat?

Can there be heartbeats just like that?

For the heart to beat, the inner force is there. Without the inner force intensity, nothing moves.

~~~

You have always taken your own existence for granted.

You only say:

'I exist because God has created me'.

This statement of yours ends here. You do not try to go behind this creation of yours.

You do not ask yourself why and what?

Why are you here?

What is there behind your own creation?

You do not ask yourself, why your heart is beating and what is behind the beats of your heart.

You do not ask yourself, why you are in action and what is behind those actions.

Go deeper within you.

Find the answers for your own existence.

~~~

When the atmosphere is calm, what really happens?

It means that Energy is in Stillness Mode.

Wind exists only when Energy is intensely pushing air towards certain direction.

DIFFERENCE BETWEEN DREAM STATE AND AWAKENED STATE

In Dream State, you become slave to the veil of ignorance. So, it is difficult at that time to differentiate between the real and the unreal. You will always be confused in the Dream State and doubt emerges. Doubt is quite apparent in this State but you should not keep on with it. Watch it intensely. By doing so, you will realize the real.

Once you start treading on the path to TRUTH, you start having glimpses of the Awakened State but then, you go back in your Dream State again.

Those glimpses are there just for you to realize how TRUTH Itself is. Some drops of the Nectar have been tasted. You should not stay with glimpses only rather your goal must be the Awakened State.

The Awakened State is where unreal does not exist, only real does. You have come out of the Dream State to find out that the real is only in the Awakened State. The Dream State has become history now. Once you are awakened, you live in the present only and the past is dead for you; the cremation has already been done.

For example, when you wake up in the morning, do you carry your sleep along with you?

NO. Once you are awake, that sleep is gone, it is dead. You cannot carry it. Now you can see only the awakened state not the sleeping one. It is the same for one who has leaped into the Awakened State, leaving the Dream State behind.

I have tried to describe it into words but I know that confusion will still be there in your mind. You will be confused because of the difference between the Mind and Beyond Mind States. It is very difficult for the limited mind to understand the Beyond Mind...

BORROWED KNOWLEDGE

Looking for the ULTIMATE meanings, in different books will not help you to understand TRUTH. TRUTH cannot be understood, IT can only be experienced. Read as many books as you wish to, but you will never understand their depth.

How can you understand that which is beyond mind?

Your understanding will be superficial. It is a waste of time. Know the TRUTH by going deeper and deeper within yourself.

When a Spiritual Master shares his Wisdom with you, he shares it depending on his state of Spiritual Evolution.

The journey of sharing Wisdom starts when one has realized the State of NO-THOUGHT and this journey does not end here.

This journey continues into different dimensions and in each dimension, the sharing of Wisdom becomes deeper.

Here, also the Spiritual Master may get stuck in one dimension for more time depending on his cleansing process.

Many people get stuck with some quotes of Wisdom. They do not know that these quotes depend on the level of evolution of the Master. When the Master goes into another dimension, the same quotes can be contradicted by him because he has changed dimensions. This is a leap to another dimension, leaving the last one behind.

You will be confused many times by the quotes of Wisdom of different Masters because they are not of the same level of evolution. Do not be confused, rather experience TRUTH yourself.

IMAGINATION

Your imagination can make you think that it is real and you keep on believing it.

There is a great difference between imagination and reality.

Imagination is only a picture that your mind configures as per your desire.

Reality is when you really find a great change within you. A transformation is going on within you, this is real.

Imagination is another veil which covers the reality.

Many times it happens that what you read in books comes back as imagination.

You think that that it is really happening to you, but in fact, it was just a dream and after some time, this dream will come to an end and you will return back to the same state as you were before. No change has happened in you. No transformation was effected.

Beware...

It is same as you think of something during the day and the same happens in your dream at night when you were sleeping.

It is only the storage of your mind reflecting in your dream.

Your desires create so many branches to veil reality that you get trapped by them very easily.

Your desires can be easily fulfilled by your imagination than in reality and that is why all your inner force is directed to them.

It is best you face reality as it is.

The only reality is whatever you experience within.

This experience transforms you as it will be increasing your awareness and at the same time, the cleansing process will eliminate the negativities found in you.

You have always chosen the easiest ways of doing things. But when it comes to treading on the path to TRUTH, you feel that it is very difficult.

There is no shortcut to TRUTH.

When treading on the path to TRUTH, you have to face reality as it comes to you every moment and if you are choosing imagination on this path, you are on the wrong track.

TRUTH cannot be made as a show-off piece.

TRUTH is TRUTH and only you know what your Truth is.

If you are using TRUTH as a show-off piece, then it is only because you wish to fulfil your desires in this way and its reaction will be very disastrous.

ATTACHMENT

Attachment is a desire which emerges from emotions. Your fear of being alone takes you to attachment. You go on attaching yourself with people, with things. You feel the need to be attached otherwise, you feel rejected. This is a feeling that takes you to such an extent.

From attachment, a chain is created:

Possessiveness
Insecurity
Jealousy
Anger
Hatred
Separation
Longing
Sufferings

The more you are attached to someone or something, the more sufferings you encounter.

When you love your dear ones, that 'love' is not there alone. It is, in fact, comprised of the above. This is the main problem.

You do not know how to love without any attachment. Wherever there is attachment, sufferings follow and you will never be free.

By meditating regularly, attachment starts dissolving gradually and once completely dissolved, that love becomes pure otherwise it remains saturated love with lots of negativities.

DETACHMENT

Example:

You go for shopping and you see a beautiful dress. You get so attracted to it that the desire of buying it arises. You finally buy it and you get attached to it that you wear it more often but it comes a time where the attachment is gone.

The dress is there in front of you but you do not enjoy wearing it anymore. There is no reaction for that dress; it is as if it does not exist for you.

This is what we call detachment. When you have no reaction with what you were attached to, you cannot enjoy it as you were doing before. Everything has changed. This is a leap from attachment to detachment.

This is an example for things that you are attached to but for human beings, it is different.

Here, love is present.

Your love for your dear ones is the one with attachment.

Love with attachment brings sufferings in return.

But you do not have to live this kind of love, instead, live it with detachment.

Your love will be the same but here, sufferings will be missing. You will love, but you will not have longing for anyone. You will not be missing anyone. You will love, but you will not have jealousy for anyone. You will love, but you will not be possessive towards anyone.

You will love freely, without any conditionings.

REFLECTION ON YOUR FACE

When you tell a lie, your eyes reflect the lie and your face too, why?

Why can't you lie the way you speak the truth?

It is just because you know from within that this is a lie and you very well know what the truth is.

What you do is, you are showing the opposite on the surface. It will definitely not work.

Your periphery and your centre must always be in tune, then, whatever you say will reflect what is within you.

You will say it with ease.

Fear makes you tell lies and lies always have bad endings.

Why not cut the root of fear itself?

Then, there will be no lies.

When you are telling a lie, firstly you are being untrue to yourself and then to others.

By just being untrue to yourself, you are doing a Negative Karma and its reaction will come back to you with greater force.

Reactions always come with intensity just to teach you a lesson.

You experience those reactions with sufferings.

FEELING CAPACITY

Your depth cannot be seen by others rather it can be felt but that also it depends on the capacity of the others' feeling.

With the increase in capacity of your feelings, your thoughts' capacity goes on decreasing. By doing this, space is being created in your mind.

Whatever it is, whether it is thoughts or feelings' capacity, your inner force is used for both.

Concentration on the feeling capacity diminishes the capacity of thoughts. The inner force is diverted to feeling and your feeling capacity starts increasing.

Wherever you divert your inner force, the capacity starts to increase. You mostly divert your inner force on thoughts, so they go on increasing and there is no space in your mind.

Every time, you wait for your thoughts to announce what you have to do. Then only you act and when you have to take decision, you take it as per what your thoughts are indicating. But do not forget that there are positive and negative thoughts.

This is why most of the time you take the wrong decisions.

Only when the mind is empty that correct decision flows directly.

The right decision that flows from an empty mind will not be a decision. It will rather be a truth and you will be acting as per truth itself.

When feeling capacity increases, there will be more and more space in your mind and then you become receptive to TRUTH.

THE PERIPHERY

Do not be attached to your periphery.

Your periphery consists of:

Fear

Anger

Jealousy

Revenge

Lust

Hatred

Superiority

Inferiority

Guilt

Go deep within yourself and find the root of all these.

You can eliminate the periphery by the dissolution of your thoughts and emotions.

This can be done only when you know how to relax.

Being relaxed does not mean that only your body is taking rest. Your thoughts and emotions also must not be there.

In this relaxed state, you are neither the physical body nor the mind.

Now that you are in this relaxed state, concentrate on your third eye.

Do not try to see anything from the third eye, just concentrate on it.

All your inner energy must be at that point of concentration.

This will activate your third eye and will make you see clearer.

Only your Consciousness is there, always in activation mode.

Be with IT as much as possible.

You are here only to accept the cleansing process for the dissolution of your thoughts and emotions.

Then only, you can come out of sufferings, in other words, you will come out from the cycle of birth and death.

You will be free forever.

In this state of FREEDOM, your periphery will be mastered by PURE CONSCIOUSNESS only.

In this FREEDOM only, you can help others who are treading on this path.

SUPPRESSION

For your own evolution, be always in tune with yourself, do not suppress.

With suppression, many problems arise and one should purify oneself by accepting the cleansing process, starting with the mind.

Why with the mind?

Your mind is always compact with thoughts. So, it is very important for you to let the cleansing happen in your mind first. Give it some space. It needs to be in a relaxed mode.

Second thing is that suppression is mostly associated with emotions.

If a desire is coming from within, watch it with detachment but do not suppress it. Watch it intensely; it will disappear on its own.

Empty yourself every day.

Whatever is there within, just share it. You can either share it with your dear ones or with Existence. The point is you have to empty yourself, do not suppress anything.

Suppression is like nourishing a volcano to erupt in the future.

The eruption of suppression makes you become more violent and you will regret after putting it into actions.

Whatever is within you, take it out. Whether it is good or bad, share it. When I say share it, I mean just express what is there within you. This expression will make you feel lighter. Suppression always erupts with anger and this is why one has to cut the root before anger appears on the surface.

BEING HELPLESS

In your past lives, you have been struggling to fulfil your desires.

The same things are continuously being repeated.

Death comes to you and you take another birth, the struggle of fulfilling all desires keeps going on.

Are you not fed up with these struggles?

Struggling is there only because you do not use your inner force for acceptance. Instead, you use it for your struggle.

You always struggle for the future because you cannot struggle for the present.

To be in the present, total acceptance of the present is needed.

You feel helpless sometimes just because things are not coming to you the way you want it to.

You are not the one who desires those things but it is your thoughts or your emotions.

When you divert your inner force towards any desire and they are not fulfilled, you feel helpless because here, you think that you have struggled so hard to fulfil that desire and yet you failed.

It is just that your inner force is not there to fulfil your desires. It is there to be used in your inner search and for you to be in actions.

Misuse of your inner force leads you to sufferings.

You are in actions by the help of your inner force. If it was not there, you and your physical body would not have been there too.

When you are helpless, you suffer within and anger emerges.

You attract more and more negativity towards you.

You start being angry with everyone who surrounds you.

What you are doing is that you feel so helpless that you wish to take it out and instead anger takes its place and comes on the periphery.

Negativity will naturally come on the surface but as an erupted volcano, with violence.

Instead, work on that helpless state of yours.

Divert your inner force to that helpless state and start watching it with intensity.

In doing so, it will start dissolving on its own.

Here, you have not allowed it to transform into anger rather you have eliminated its root.

When it has completely dissolved, you will be in a lighter mode, relaxed.

Never suppress any emotion, rather watch with intensity until it is completely dissolved.

ACCEPTANCE

For you to understand something, you have to accept it first.

Acceptance itself will create a space in you and you will be able to come to a deeper understanding but if that acceptance is not there, then understanding also is dead.

Once understanding is dead for you, your ego increases.

It is very easy to talk about acceptance but are you really accepting what is true?

The more you ignore TRUTH, the greater you will suffer.

You may not show your sufferings to the periphery now, but these sufferings will torment you so much that you will be so helpless and eventually you will have to accept TRUTH.

You have no choice.

TRUTH is TRUTH.

You take time to accept TRUTH; the longer you take, the more you suffer.

Example:

When a third person comes in between a husband and his wife, a lot of problems arise in the couple's life. It causes a lot of misunderstandings.

Sincerity is not there anymore.

Trust is not there anymore.

Love is not there anymore.

A barrier is created between the two.

Similarly, the third one is thoughts and emotions coming in between you and your actions.

You make many mistakes in life but that does not mean that you are inferior.

In fact, you learn from each mistake and that lesson is what counts the most.

That lesson transforms you and makes you grow up.

The transformation is of understanding.

The lesson takes you to a deeper understanding.

After that deep understanding, you will not commit the same mistake again.

You do not have to feel guilty about the past mistakes, you have to instead, enjoy what you are in the present.

Guilt comes from emotions. You feel that when you have made a mistake, it is the greatest mistake and it is not forgivable.

NO.

You made that mistake just because you were not in tune with yourself and you can compensate for that only by being in tune with yourself in the present.

By mourning over the past mistakes, you are making yourself weak.

Weakness attracts more negativity towards you and thus, your sufferings go on increasing.

The day you accept that guilt is of the past and decide not to carry it with you anymore, you will experience an inner strength and you will start attracting positivity.

Be true to yourself first, then, accept every Truth that comes to you.

There are two journeys:

The Ego Journey

The Inner Journey

The Ego Journey takes you to negativity and the Inner Journey to positivity.

Most of the time, people get drowned in the Ego Journey and it requires great courage to move from the Ego journey to the Inner Journey.

The Inner Journey seems endless to you just because you get carried away by the Ego Journey very easily.

The Ego Journey takes you to a dream world and the Inner Journey shows you all that is REAL...

Leave the unreal and welcome the real...

SURRENDER

Surrender means that you are ready to let go of your Ego.

That let go is of great importance.

Ego is that negativity that needs to be dissolved. The more you nourish your Ego, the greater sufferings you welcome. To bring your Ego to dissolution, you will have to accept the cleansing process. Let this process purify you totally.

When you start surrendering, you become receptive of TRUTH and this receptivity itself is welcoming blessings on its own.

Here, it depends how long your surrendering is for.

If you surrender for one minute, you will receive blessings for that length of period only. The longer you surrender, the more you absorb.

When you are surrendering, you are not surrendering to anyone. You are not surrendering to God or to a Guru or to a Spiritual Master.

You are, in fact, gradually surrendering your Ego and space is created within you to absorb TRUTH.

This is also a give and take. You give your space and you absorb TRUTH.

When the womb of TRUTH explodes by your growth, all your identities are dissolved.

You become TRUTH Itself, without any title.

LOVE

There is a great difference between physical attraction and love.

Many people consider physical attraction to be love itself and consequently they do not come to a deep understanding.

Love can bring you to deep understanding but one has to go in love deeper and deeper.

Physical attraction is just the periphery. With periphery you will never come to deep understanding.

Love in itself is beautiful but when it is mixed with ego, it is saturated.

Love is like a pool which you have to keep on digging.

As you dig deeper and deeper, deep understanding emerges from it.

When you are in love, you have a longing for meeting the other.

When the wish is there, you are always in the urge of fulfilling it.

You do not try to find out what that wish is, where it comes from and what is there behind this feeling.

The treasure is not found on the periphery but rather in the centre.

So, go profoundly within, with infinite patience.

Infinite patience will bring you closer to yourself.

The closer you are to yourself, the more intimate you will be with your partner.

Being in love is also an emotion and the longing associated with it brings suffering to you.

Longing is desire mixed with sufferings.

You need to have infinite patience, only then you can work on yourself.

Always be a spontaneous lover, without any conditioning, without any longing.

Just being in love is beautiful.

Do not attach anything to it.

When you are in love, you feel that everything that surrounds you is beautiful.

At that specific moment, you become more loving and you radiate this love to your surroundings.

Here, your fragrance is in tune with Existence.

Enjoy these moments to the fullest.

DESIRES

People keep on complaining that 'It is not happening' on the path to TRUTH.

There must be space within you for it to happen.

How do you know it is not happening?

Is it just because your desires are not being fulfilled?

Then you are on the wrong track.

The path to TRUTH is not for fulfilling desires. This path is for eliminating your desires till you have no desire left.

Expectation is a desire combined with attachment.

When your expectation is not fulfilled, anger comes on the surface.

When your expectation is fulfilled, another expectation pops in and it goes on like this; it is a never ending process.

You have to put a full stop to this process of desires by accepting the cleansing process.

Everyone is taking part in a competition; a competition of fulfilling desires.

In this competition, everyone is attracting suffering just because they have desires to satisfy.

Example:

The bud is there. It has two choices; it can either blossom or attract insects.

The same are the choices for you, you can either accept the cleansing process and blossom or you can attract negativity and suffer.

HAPPINESS

Happiness is energy mixed with your fulfilled desires. When your desires are satisfied, you feel happy for some instant only. At that time, you know you are happy but it is not a deep happiness. It is happiness on the periphery, a temporary one. That happiness is not permanent.

Once another desire comes on the surface, the happiness is gone and a longing for the other desire to be fulfilled comes up.

That urge of fulfilling desires itself takes your time and energy and you can go to any extreme level to achieve this fulfilment.

This is where you go wrong.

You are not here to use your inner force for this purpose; it has to be used for a deeper understanding. When deep understanding gradually increases, happiness too will increase. When happiness increases, it will come to you without any reason.

Accepting the cleansing process is your priority in life. The cleansing process dissolves your desires gradually. After that you will realise that you are happy but you do not know the reason why. Happiness will be there continuously as if a celebration is going on.

Later with more cleansing, you will reach a State where you neither feel happy nor sad, that is, you come to a Stillness mode.

Everything is happening on the periphery but you are just watching the periphery without being affected by either happiness or sadness. This is where you are not dependent on both thoughts and emotions.

You have gone beyond both. This is the Pure State.

MOTHER

The inner force that a mother uses to give birth to her baby is the same inner force that is there in you.

Have you ever asked yourself that at the time of creation, where does that force come from?

The time when a mother comes to know that she is expecting a baby, her inner force starts increasing.

It is so only because the mother's attention is more on the expected baby than anything else.

The inner force intensity increases gradually for the baby to grow.

Here also space is needed for the baby to grow properly.

This space has been created by the mother's constant concentration at the navel centre.

It becomes very natural for her to watch there but she does not know that she is at the same time practising a meditation technique.

A mother, normally, takes more rest in the state of pregnancy. She will feel exhausted very quickly. She cannot do the same amount of activities that she was doing before.

It is just because the physical body has to be in a resting mode for growth to happen.

When her physical body is in a resting mode, she is available to absorb more energy for both, herself and the baby. The more energy she absorbs, the healthier both will be.

Creation happens in Supreme Silence and Darkness.

If that inner force can make creation happen, then what about your inner force?

It has always been said that men are the strongest but what about women?

In fact, both have the same strength.

The only difference is that men use their strength on outer things and women in the inner.

Women's strength is used for creation.

So, never underestimate anyone. Everyone has the same strength, the same inner force.

For creation to happen, intensity of Energy is needed for the explosion.

When the mother is about to deliver her baby, she gathers a lot of courage and energy to give birth to that child.

She is even surprised where this courage has come from all of a sudden.

She is unaware of the fact that when she was carrying the baby for nine months, she was watchful and this watchfulness was the preparation of the physical body to welcome the explosion during delivery.

Many times, you are watchful but you do not know it is helping you within.

If explosion and creation can happen by being watchful unknowingly, then just imagine the effect when you are being watchful with awareness.

Experience it and KNOW.

COMPASSION

What is Compassion?

Compassion emerges from emotion.

The process is like this:

Love after being refined = Compassion

Compassion after being refined = Stillness Mode

Compassion is pure love. When one is compassionate, it means that he or she is ready to help others without any discrimination. He or she starts devoting his or her life for others rather than for himself or herself.

But do not forget, Compassion is still an emotion. A person who is compassionate still has feelings and sheds tears.

The inner journey does not end with Compassion. Compassion has to be refined again and after being refined, one comes to a State of Stillness, where one has no feelings at all. Here, emotion box has disappeared.

He or she has become PURE CONSCIOUSNESS Itself.

Does Energy have Compassion?

Does Silence have Compassion?

Similarly, the SOURCE does not have Compassion.

Compassion is only for those who are still attached to emotions. Those who have Compassion are still in the process of cleansing.

LESSONS

You learn the lesson of Life by experiencing life not by reading about life.

You learn the lesson of Death by experiencing death not by reading about death.

You learn the lesson of Love by experiencing love not by reading about love.

You learn the lesson of Bliss by experiencing bliss not by reading about bliss.

You learn the lesson of Peace by experiencing peace not by reading about peace.

You learn the lesson of Surrendering by experiencing surrender not by reading about surrender.

You learn the lesson of Faith by experiencing faith not by reading about faith.

You learn the lesson of Gratitude by experiencing gratitude not by reading about gratitude.

When you have experienced all, only then you can come to a State where you stop experiencing.

You have become 'YOU' from 'you'.

Only 'you' can experience, 'YOU' cannot experience.

'YOU' only radiate.

You stopped experiencing only when 'you' have dissolved forever and only 'YOU' are.

'YOU' are 'THE ALL KNOWING' and when YOU know all, happenings too stop, then, 'THE ALL KNOWING' flows everywhere.

Happenings are still there when 'you' are coming closer to 'YOU' and when 'you' has dissolved completely, then only 'YOU' remain, happenings cease.

SEPARATION

In between you and the other, there is LOVE.

In between you and the other, there is COMPASSION.

In between you and the other, there is ENMITY.

In between you and the other, there is EGO.

In between you and the other, there is HATRED.

In between you and the other, there is ANGER.

In between you and the other, there is UNCONDITIONAL LOVE.

In between you and the other, there is SUPERIORITY.

In between you and the other, there is JEALOUSY.

In between you and the other, there is DESIRE.

In between you and the other, there is LUST.

In between you and the other, there is REVENGE.

Accept the cleansing process and let these barriers be dropped.

DIVERSION OF THOUGHTS AND EMOTIONS

You do actions under the guidance of your thoughts and emotions.

You use your inner force to put your thoughts and emotions into actions; here I am referring to anger, lust, revenge, jealousy.

Only the diversion of your inner force makes the difference. Either you choose to divert it on the periphery where sufferings are awaiting you or you divert it to the Source where you come to merge with TRUTH.

All the scriptures in the past and present are showing you the way how to be to the Source but you are learning them by heart instead of treading that path.

The way thoughts come on its own in your mind, Wisdom also flows on its own in your mind. But if you do not make space in your mind to let Wisdom flow, your thoughts will always master you.

Wisdom flows only when you are not dependent on thoughts and emotions, that is, when you are totally empty.

Example:

The Sun is you and its radiance is Wisdom.

Have you ever noticed that when you are absorbed in any activity you love, you forget yourself and only that activity exists?

Yes, there is love combined with that activity, but you are not there, why?

It is only because at that time you were more concerned with that activity rather than your thoughts. In this way, thoughts are absent and emptiness took its place.

Do this with every action of yours.

You can also divert your thoughts by watching your emotions. Then, your mind will be empty and the emotions will start dissolving.

Here, what happens, you are working on both, thoughts and emotions.

Both thoughts and emotions will start dissolving on their own and you will be freed from them gradually.

The Steps

First step is diverting thoughts, thus, gradual dissolution of thoughts at the same time.

Second step is the dissolution of emotions.

Third step is deep relaxation.

What is left is Actions, in deep relaxation.

www.ingramcontent.com/pod-product-compliance
Lightning Source LLC
Chambersburg PA
CBHW071311040426
42444CB00009B/1974